D1565177

THE SIAMESE FIGHTING FISH:
its life cycle

This large size mature male has mixed blue and red coloration. Fins are spread in partial display.

colorful
nature
series

THE SIAMESE
FIGHTING FISH:
its life cycle

THE BETTA AND PARADISE FISH

597
W
8232

By William White, Jr., Ph.D

STERLING PUBLISHING CO., INC. NEW YORK

Oak Tree Press Co., Ltd. London & Sydney

COLORFUL NATURE SERIES

The Guppy: Its Life Cycle   The Penguin: Its Life Cycle
The Siamese Fighting Fish: Its Life Cycle

STERLING NATURE SERIES

Ant Is Born	Hidden Life of Flowers
Bee Is Born	Secret Life of Small Animals
Bird Is Born	Silkworm Is Born
Birds That Fly in the Night	Tiny Living Things
Butterfly Is Born	Tree Grows Up
Fern Is Born	Tree Is Born
Frog Is Born	Turtle Is Born
Fruit Is Born	

Acknowledgments

The author and publisher wish to thank Dr. & Mrs. James Böhlke of the Academy of Natural Sciences of Philadelphia for their numerous excellent suggestions concerning Anabantoids, Ms. Diane M. Farny for her bibliographical research into several hundred technical papers, and to Rebecca L. White for preparing the manuscript.

Contents

Illus. 1. This exceptionally large light-hued male with blue fins is an example of the "cornflower" variety of Betta.

Introduction

The Siamese Fighting Fish, *Betta splendens*, and its close relative the Paradise Fish, *Macropodus opercularis*, are members of the small sub-order of fishes called Anabantoidei or Anabantoids. The origin of this scientific name is the Greek verb, *anabaino*, meaning "to journey up" or "to go up." This refers to the habit these fishes have of swimming to the surface every minute or so to inhale fresh air and exhale exhausted air. These little fish are not only provided with the usual gills, but they have an accessory breathing mechanism (or labyrinth) which permits them to breathe atmospheric oxygen directly.

Their brilliant crimson and royal blue coloration, their deliberate movements and the courtly combats in mating, have excited the imaginations of generations of aquarists, and the peoples of Southeast Asia have kept the Siamese Fighting Fish in captivity for centuries. The male fish are matched in contests and spectators wager on the outcomes. Especially ferocious specimens command high prices and draw high wagers. The Fighting Fish is correctly named for it is actually a native of Thailand, the modern name of Siam.

The Betta is the most ferocious of all aquarium fishes, as it will nearly always attack and many times kill another Betta of the same sex. This is 99 per cent true of males and about 45 per cent true of females. The Paradise will nip and pester members of its own species, but is rarely a true killer fish.

Illus. 2. It is the slime coat-ing on its sides which catches and refracts light. The Betta has very few of the iridocytes of bony fishes.

Illus. 3. A large male Paradise Fish, fully 4 years old and heavy-bodied, shows its breeding colors. These fish will spawn at 3 inches, but are full grown at 4½ inches.

Illus. 4. This mature red/tan male Betta has highlights flashing on its fins.

Illus. 5. This tan/red female is nearly indistinguishable from preserved specimens of the original wild type of Betta.

Both the Betta and the Paradise have a combination of characteristics which make them ideal aquarium pets. With some attention to preparations and some adequate-size tanks, nearly any amateur aquarist can keep and spawn these attracttive fishes. They have an incredible resistance to bad water and cramped quarters and can withstand a wide range of temperature variations. The Paradise Fish is easier to keep than the Betta and the males will not fight. However, males

9

Illus. 6. A ghostly yellow variety of the pale red/tan strain called "Cambodian" Bettas. A true albino Betta is exceedingly rare and all attempts to get albino specimens to reproduce have failed. Albino Paradise Fish, however, have been successfully bred.

and females of both species should be kept separate to prevent bullying. A single pair of either species will go nicely in a community tank of larger fish with at least 40 gallons (150 litres) capacity.

The Betta and the Paradise Fish are important members of a fish family which has the accessory breathing organ. Using this organ, they have developed the elaborate breeding habits shown later in this book, but usually simply called bubble-nest building.

Their habit of fin-nipping has at times cast the Betta and the Paradise in less than a popular light. However, the secret of keeping peace is to afford them sufficient space. The males will usually hide behind a filter tube or vertical heating element, and on some occasions fill the small area with a fine thick bubble nest.

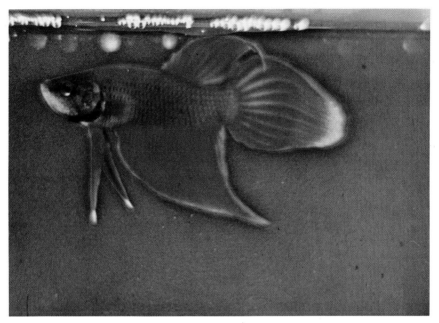

Illus. 7. The classic red male Betta shows a partial display.

I. Anatomy

Part of the fascination of keeping the Betta and Paradise is noting the incredible way their anatomy is adapted to their environment, especially their accessory breathing organ. This affects and involves their whole complex breeding, nest building, and rearing of their young. Many, many questions are yet to be answered about the Betta, the Paradise, and their relatives among the Anabantoids. In the following pages, an attempt will be made to state and answer some of them.

The *Betta splendens* is small among the Anabantoids. The

11

Illus. 8. In this head of a large male Betta, note how the mouth is set at a slant toward the water surface.

males reach a length of about $2\frac{3}{8}$ inches (6 cm.) with the females somewhat smaller, 2 inches (5.5 cm.), lacking the long flowing fins of the male. The dorsal fin contains one stiff and 8 to 9 soft rays, the anal fin 2 to 4 stiff and 21 to 24 soft rays. The count of scales along the lateral axis varies between 30 and 32. The head is characteristic of the Anabantoids with a slightly undershot lower jaw and the prominent eyes which appear to be the fishes' most important sense organs.

Unlike land animals, fishes do not hear sound waves passing through air but must sense pressure waves passing through water. Smell consists of detecting water-borne particles, but there is no evidence that this yields any information on the direction of food or danger as it does in land animals.

The mouth of the Betta serves as do the forelimbs of land animals. Not only is it the grasping and shearing organ for food, but also the grasping organ for mating rituals, capture and care of eggs and young, and the chief weapon of offense and defense. The Betta feeds in the middle levels of the water in its natural habitat and goes on up to the surface, so its mouth aligns on an upward slant.

Food passes through the fish's mouth and pharynx, guided by the bone-supported tongue and on into the digestive tract.

12

Illus. 9. In this enlarged view of the head, the small depressions on the front surface above the mouth are the openings of smell and pressure sensitive organs.

gill filaments   accessory breathing organ   orbit   eye   nostril

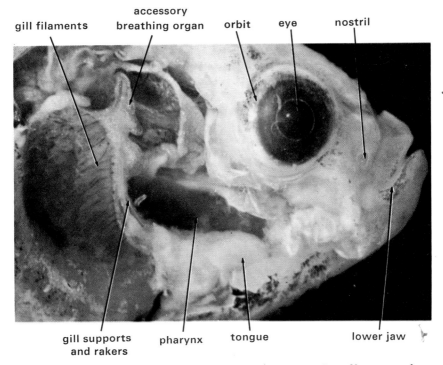

gill supports and rakers   pharynx   tongue   lower jaw

Illus. 10. This large male has been partly dissected to show the location of the pharynx, tongue, gill rakers, gill filaments, and accessory breathing organ in the area of the head.

13

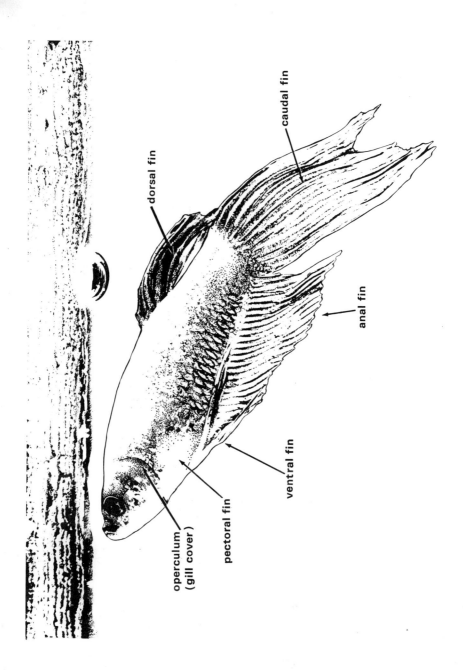

dorsal fin

caudal fin

anal fin

ventral fin

pectoral fin

operculum
(gill cover)

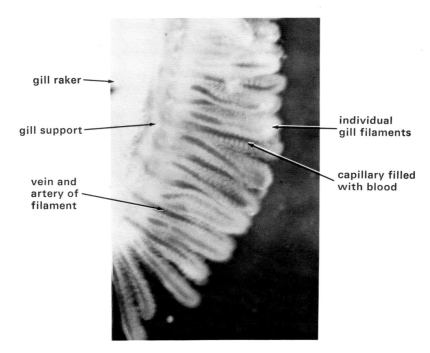

gill raker

gill support

vein and
artery of
filament

individual
gill filaments

capillary filled
with blood

Illus. 11. Gill raker, gills, and gill filaments are filled with oxygen-rich blood.

The other important function of the Betta's elaborate muscle and valve system is to pass fresh water carrying dissolved oxygen over the gills. These are actually elaborate antenna-like frames which provide the broadest possible surface contact for the fish's circulatory system, so that oxygen-depleted blood can give up carbon dioxide and take on oxygen.

The gills have the first bony support or arch expanded into a sac-like organ shaped into bracket-like layers. This arrangement is supported by cartilages called lamellae. This sac with its many folds and loops is the accessory breathing or labyrinth organ, and because of this the Anabantoids are also called labyrinth fishes.

15

The Labyrinth Tested

There has been a great deal of discussion among aquarists about the relationship between the gills and the accessory organ of Anabantoids. It is well known that Bettas and Paradise Fish can survive extreme crowding. (The author has kept one for extended periods up to 15 days in an 8-ounce drinking glass.) They can also survive foul, polluted water when other fishes kept with them have died. But do these fish depend upon the accessory organ only when the regular dissolved oxygen supply is depleted?

To find an answer, the author designed and built a clear enclosure that would prevent the fish from coming up to the surface for fresh air. This enclosure had 1-cm. holes drilled through the sides and top. Both Bettas and Paradise were put

Illus. 12. The accessory breathing organ in a freshly preserved specimen shows that the membranes of the sac (very red) are filled with newly oxygenated blood. The surgical probe holds the organ out away from the spine to show blood-perfused tissues. Frequently, when the organ of a preserved specimen is shown, the fullness and membraneous character of the tissue is not obvious.

in and the apparatus was sunk to the bottom of a standard aquarium of 20 gallons (80 litres) and later a standard aquarium of 100 gallons (400 litres). At least 25 different Bettas and 10 different Paradise were tested in the enclosure, one at a time, with other fishes swimming around the outside of the enclosure. All were timed, and there was no possible way for them to breathe except through the gill mechanism. The top of the enclosure allowed free currents of water, but kept the fish 10 inches (25 cm.) from the surface in the 20-gallon tank and 24 inches (63 cm.) in the 100-gallon tank. In all cases the fishes showed marked respiratory difficulty within from 5 to 10 minutes.

Since this was only a trial and far from being a controlled scientific experiment, only a few speculations can be made. To protect from outright water problems which might go undetected within the enclosure, goldfish were put into the enclosure in many cases with the specimen being tested. No goldfish either altered its activity or died.

Two types of activity resulted in this trial. Some Paradise and nearly all Bettas (both males and females) became extremely apprehensive at their inability to reach the surface. After a period of wild thrashing against the top of the enclosure they would begin to grow stiff and fall on their sides at the bottom of the enclosure with gills distended and pumping abnormally hard and rapidly. If not released to swim directly to the surface for an exchange of air, they quickly died. Most of the Paradise and some (usually female) Bettas would lie on the bottom without the mad dashing. This apparently reduced their biological oxygen requirement and they would survive this way for fairly long periods. In fact, one lived through a 12-hour period this way.

The accessory organ seems to be an integral part of the

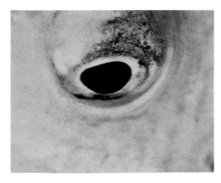

Illus. 13. From the first week after hatching, the large eye of the Betta can be moved outward on its axis to give very good perspective vision.

fishes' respiratory mechanism. Either by physiology or behavioral conditioning, few specimens are able to survive for very long without its use. The development of the accessory organ seems to be incomplete, and so the fish is left in a developmental "middle ground." In this sense, the accessory organ is a partially "missing link." It is not as developed as the breathing mechanism of those Anabantoids which can leave the water, specifically, the Climbing Perch. However, the accessory organ certainly serves the purpose of allowing the Betta and Paradise to use atmospheric air.

Gills and Other Organs of the Head

The often-repeated statement that the Betta and Paradise can drown, is partially true. The Betta and Paradise utilize their gills so much that they can deplete the oxygen supply in tanks. Although they can exist for a time in cramped space, they need just as much room for living space as any other similar-sized aquarium fish, especially as fry, because the development of the accessory breathing apparatus comes much later than that of the gill apparatus in the sixth to tenth week after hatching.

Beneath and behind the accessory breathing organ on each side of the spine are the directional organs of the Betta and

18

Paradise Fish. It is vitally important for all motile animals to be able to orient themselves, up, down, back, forth, right, and left. In higher forms, the inner ear serves to associate the sense of balance with hearing. In bony fishes an otolithic (meaning "earstone") organ develops very early. The Betta and the Paradise actually secrete calcium carbonate derived from their environment within a tiny hard-walled sac filled with fluid. This sac does not change its shape or position, but it is lined with hair-like nerve endings. The liths or stones move within the fluid. As the fish moves in any direction the inertia causes the "earstones" to exert slight pressure on the nerve endings and this is interpreted by the fish's brain as an indication of direction.

The shapes of these tiny liths are so specific to species and genera that an experienced observer can identify a species from a single otolith only a few millimeters in length.

Since the Betta and Paradise are both predators feeding on live animal material in or at the surface of the water, the eye is one of the most sensitive of their sense organs. It begins to form a bare 12 hours after the eggs are fertilized. The eye is capable of both monocular-vision—one eye focussed on a different object than the other—and binocular-vision—both eyes focussed on the same object. The lens of the Betta's eye is hard and fibrous, and is, of course, adapted for vision in water.

Repeated experimentation has shown that both the Betta and the Paradise have some sort of color vision. Neither Betta nor Paradise does well when kept in total darkness nor can it survive very low light levels for long periods of time. These fish are quiet and move very little at night. The Paradise will spawn in mildly subdued light; the Betta will not, as it must have a fair exposure to light to do well in captivity.

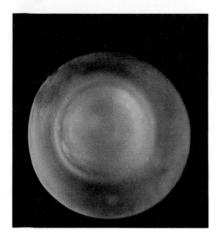

Illus. 14. The round lens of the Betta eye contains finely spun rows of protein-based fibres which can just barely be discerned. The lens has two distinct layers, an outer shell and an inner sphere. The result is a 4-element lens, which focusses the incoming light and the image upon the retina, the bundle of light-sensitive nerve endings at the back of the eye.

This proves that color signals are important in the Betta's behavior.

The nervous system of the Betta and Paradise is similar to most bony fishes. The optic lobe (portion of the brain concerned with sight) and cerebellum (main brain area) are of nearly equal size, while the olfactory bulbs (smell organs) are drawn out toward the front of the head. This structure indicates that visual cues, such as movement and color, are detected by the eye and bring about a rapid instinctive response, rather than any deductive or thinking action. The spinal chord passes through the middle of the vertebra to the tail.

Some ichthyologists have concluded that the Paradise is somewhat more developed in the bone structure of its head than the Betta. The skulls of bony fishes are extremely variable from species to species and fitted very precisely to their environment and ecology. The Betta head is no exception.

olfactory　olfactory　optic　trochlear　acoustic　　　　　　　　medulla
nerve　　　lobe　　lobe　　nerve　　nerve　　cerebellum　oblongata

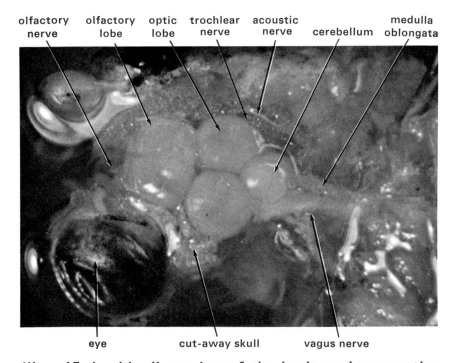

eye　　　　　　cut-away skull　　　vagus nerve

Illus. 15. In this dissection of the brain and connecting nerves of a large male Betta, not only the eye, optic nerve, optic lobe, cerebellum, and medulla oblongata can be seen, but also some of the 12 cranial nerves are visible.

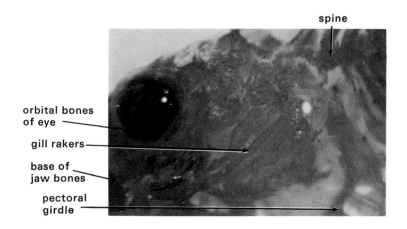

spine

orbital bones
of eye

gill rakers

base of
jaw bones

pectoral
girdle

Illus. 16. The Betta skull, stained red, shows all fine bones which give the jaw its tremendous power. The gill rakers are visible along with the axis, the first few vertebrae and the top portion of the pectoral or shoulder girdle, which supports the pectoral fins.

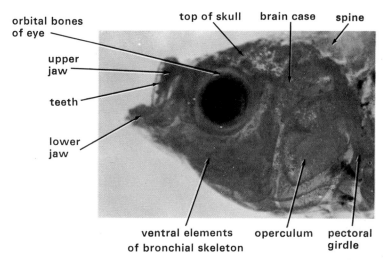

orbital bones
of eye

top of skull   brain case   spine

upper
jaw

teeth

lower
jaw

ventral elements
of bronchial skeleton

operculum   pectoral
girdle

Illus. 17. The Betta skull shows the jaws, eye and orbit, large gill cover-plates (operculum), and complete pectoral girdle.

Illus. 18. The teeth of the Betta's lower jaw, with the bite curved inward, provides for easy capture of prey. The prey, as in almost all predatory fishes, is swallowed whole.

Illus. 19. The Betta's lower jaw, with its hooking teeth, can be extended to snare prey. It is this mouth arrangement, as awesome for its size as any tiger's, which gives the Betta its deadly fighting technique.

23

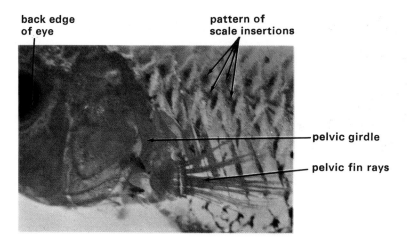

back edge
of eye

pattern of
scale insertions

pelvic girdle

pelvic fin rays

Illus. 20. In looking at the color pattern of the middle segment of the Betta body, the way the scales are inserted can be observed.

Coloration

The Betta varies from dark red/purple through tans and orange/browns to a light yellow. Light pink specimens do occur, but albino (colorless) specimens are very rare. The dominant colors are always reds and blues. A layer of tissue which has color-bearing cells, or chromophores, in it, covers the scales.

All Paradise Fish have a red stripe against some blueish background. Some specimens will have a brown marking or margin along the dark bars. The albino variety has a suffuse pink or salmon background. A variety of Paradise with a more general blue is called the concolor. The albino variety

Illus. 21. A small segment of skin from a large male Betta has been enlarged here to show the distribution of color-bearing cells or chromophores. Almost all Bettas have the same colors, the difference in the net effect being due to the density of the chromophores as they lay over one another.

can be gentler than the standard and the concolor is likely to be more irritable. The concolor will interbreed with the standard, but the albino will rarely do so without both fishes being in peak preparation for spawning.

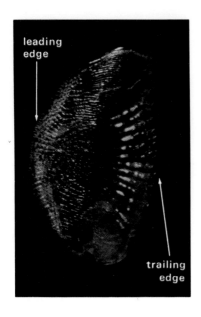

leading
edge

trailing
edge

Illus. 22. A single nearly translucent ctenoid type scale shows the rough tooth-like trailing edges. Scales are made up of thin layers of bone with fibres and crystals embedded in them. The scales give off and reflect a marvelous array of colors. In patterns they give the Betta its subtle shadings.

The Skeleton and Internal Organs

The skeleton of the Betta and Paradise is similar to all other bony fishes, aside from the special adaptations of the bones of the head.

The Betta has 29 vertebrae in its spinal column, 10 in the trunk region where the viscera and respiratory organs are located, and the rest in the back and tail region. The Paradise has from 26 to 28 vertebrae, 9 in the trunk region, with from 17 to 19 in the back and tail.

The Paradise is a larger fish than the Betta, about average in length and weight for an Anabantoid. Fully mature males may reach $4\frac{1}{2}$ inches (11 cm.), but most are mature and will spawn at about 3 inches. The females may be nearly as big, but are heavier in the anal region. They lack the extensive fins

Illus. 23. The skeleton of the Paradise, stained and slightly cleared, shows the heavy bones that support the head muscles which operate the jaws and gills, and the many ribs and rays which support the swimming muscles and fins.

and bright coloration of the males. The dorsal fin contains 13 to 14 stiff rays and 6 to 8 soft rays, the anal 17 to 20 stiff and 11 to 15 soft rays, the ventral one stiff and 5 soft rays. The count of scales along the lateral axis varies from 28 to 31. The sex distinctions in the Paradise are not as prominent as those in the Betta, and develop later in the young fish.

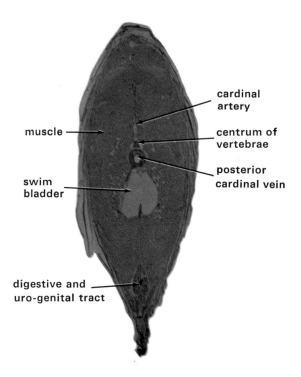

muscle

swim
bladder

cardinal
artery

centrum of
vertebrae

posterior
cardinal vein

digestive and
uro-genital tract

*Illus. 24. Cross section of the caudal or tail region of the
Betta. The large opening in the middle is the back portion
of the swim bladder, and immediately above is a vertebra. The compressed membranes at the bottom are the
anal fin.*

The internal organs of the Betta and Paradise are standard
for a small perch-like fresh-water fish. They eat very little
plant material, the Paradise taking plant material more often
than the Betta.

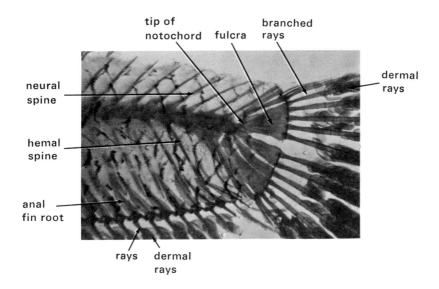

tip of notochord   fulcra   branched rays

dermal rays

neural spine

hemal spine

anal fin root

rays   dermal rays

Illus. 25. Skeleton of the caudal fin area shows the spine with vertebrae, caudal supports, and dermal rays in the flowing tail.

Their short digestive tract is fitted for animal matter which they eat in abundance. Stomach contents of specimens caught in the wild show much the same fare that they prefer in the aquarium. They feed on vast numbers of insect larvae in their native habitat.

The most popular foods with both the Betta and the Paradise are small fresh-water crustaceans and aquatic insects. In the aquarium, they are among the few fishes that will systematically destroy snails.

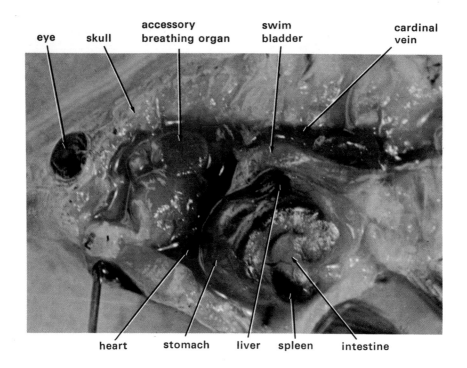

eye   skull   accessory breathing organ   swim bladder   cardinal vein

heart   stomach   liver   spleen   intestine

Illus. 26. The internal organs of a large male Betta.

Surprisingly enough, neither the Betta nor the Paradise seems to prefer smaller fishes. Even 10-day-old Anabantoids will stalk and seize prey rather than pursue it. Although capable of short bursts of intense speed, Anabantoids are usually slow-moving and must be specially fed when in community tanks with fast swimming fishes, or they will suffer from the competition for food.

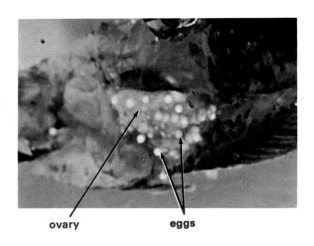

Illus. 27. The ovaries of a large female Betta have been dissected to show quantity of eggs in all stages of maturation.

ovary   eggs

Swimming

The swimming of the Betta and Paradise is of two types. When not in danger of pursuit, they paddle along with their nearly transparent pectoral fins. The tail is symmetrical above and below the midline. Betta and Paradise both have neutral buoyancy, which they maintain with their swim bladders. These transparent sacs, located behind the gills, are filled with gas which ultimately is suffused into the blood. The swim bladder contains oxygen, nitrogen, and such rare gases as argon and helium. This gaseous organ keeps the fish's weight at near zero in water. The tail can act as a rudder or brake against the force of the current churned by the ever-moving pectorals. When the fish is frightened or must make a final swift dash in pursuit of food, its swimming becomes much more rapid. The broad surface of its tail may be flipped in one great S-shaped or sinusoidal movement along with the body to greatly accelerate its speed.

Illus. 28. Two mature males approach to identify each other, and attempt intimidation. The blue male is showing this is his territory being invaded by making a partial display with raised dorsal, anal, and caudal fins. His blue-and-red rival does likewise.

2. Behavior

In studying Anabantoids, it is fascinating to follow their complex behavior. Three different patterns can be discerned: (1) ways they protect their territory; (2) ways they battle for sexual supremacy over competing males; and (3) actions they take in courting, nest building and rearing their young.

Territorial protection is practiced by the Betta to an extreme, and only slightly by the Paradise. The Betta male in

Illus. 29. Blue's partial display has failed, and the blue-and-red opponent keeps coming on. So the blue male turns sharply to ward off an attack at his mid-section. This causes a circling procession, a basic feature in Betta combats, to begin. After more circling at a slow and very cautious pace, head to tail, four or five times around, counter-clockwise, the bout breaks off while both males breathe at the surface. Males tend to breathe more frequently during combats, but both take their inhalations at the same time as if by tradition.

possession in a close enclosure, on sighting another male, will flare his fins and raise his gill covers in a wavering side-to-side display. This goes on until he drives off the aggressor or interloper. Two males, even when separated by a glass, will follow each other along in the same direction, each undulating with all fins spread in display.

In seeking sexual supremacy over competing males, both

Illus. 30. When the blue male comes back to circle again, he makes a full display, and now has the advantage for attack. The red-blue declines to compete in full display, folds his gill covers, and moves off. Blue is now victor and in full control of both territory and any waiting females.

the Betta and the Paradise Fish will engage in such combats in a tank of mixed males and females. Small, young males are often killed, and injured males seldom survive. The male will make careful head-first attacks on its opponent and open its jaws for a tearing bite during such a lunge.

Full-force killing assaults of Bettas are aimed at two points: against the side of the opponent around the gill plate or at the upper head. The usual cause of death seems to be respiratory failure brought on by the shock and tissue loss in the attack. A few strong biting attacks usually are sufficient to kill a victim.

34

Illus. 31. Not all the combats end with success after a mere ritual display and feigning of combat. In this battle, the stronger and older male, the lower fish, got a deadly jaw lock on his smaller opponent. He will hold him there at this unnatural angle until his rival succumbs.

On rare occasions, the author has seen a killer-female. These Amazons usually tear the tail or pectoral fin off their victim, and then when the victim's activities are slowed down, they destroy the breathing apparatus.

Courting and nest building activities follow as a result of the successful defense of territory and the securing of supremacy over rival males. Males and females of the same basic coloring seem to be more attracted to each other, and it has been shown that males of the same color tend to fight more readily. This simply means that dull or diverse colored males do not mate as easily. The very few albino Bettas that have appeared have been virtually impossible to breed. The follow-

Illus. 32. A mature red male Betta is fashioning his bubble nest. He merely needs to blow groups of bubbles into the middle of the nest and they spread out on the water surface. The bubbles are sticky from a cement that comes with the air from the Betta's mouth.

ing steps in the mating process are common to Betta and Paradise with few exceptions.

First, a bubble nest is built. The male of both species blows air through his mouth in such a way that it picks up some secretion from a set of cement glands in his mouth. Their mixture comes out as bubbles which are adhesive and surprisingly long-lasting. Because of their stickiness, the bubbles adhere to fine floating plants and other debris at the surface

36

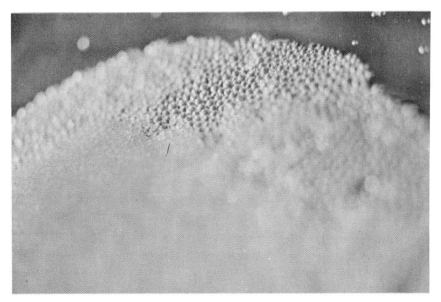

Illus. 33. Looking at the surface of a 6-inch-wide bubble nest from above the aquarium, the double- and triple-thick layers of bubbles seem lighter in shade.

and incorporate them into the bubble nest. It is normal for almost all male Bettas and a good many Paradise Fish to make nests at the surface in any container in which they are kept. When females are visible to the males, the nest building will be accelerated. The same thing will occur when the temperature is raised to the normal breeding range, 77–86° F. (25–30° C.). The Paradise will nest and court at some degrees lower, but the Betta will not be successful at any cooler temperature. The best water depth for spawning has been variously reported as 8 inches (21 cm.), but the author has found better results with half as much water. A surface area of 150 square inches (600 sq. cm.) is even more important. Most important of all is a very tight-fitting glass cover.

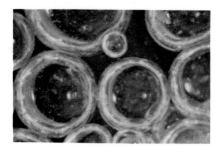

Illus. 34. A low-power photomicrograph of a small portion of a bubble nest shows the variation in size of the bubbles.

After the nest is well underway, the male is ready to court a willing female. Usually the nest itself is a visual cue and most females, when full of mature eggs and ready to spawn, will swim under it willingly. If they are too young, in poor condition or sexually inexperienced, females will often flee from the nest area. This usually results in hot pursuit by the male and may end in a vicious attack upon the female. This is the crucial point to watch in aquarium spawnings of these fishes. If, for some reason, the female does not take up a

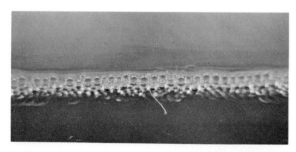

Illus. 35. Looking through the edge at the water surface, you can see how a bubble nest holds small pieces of organic materials on its mass of floating bubbles.

position under or around the male while he guards the nest, then she must be removed or placed in a separate compartment within the breeding tank or she may be destroyed. The author has had success in saving the female by inserting across the tank a sheet of clear plastic with holes just large enough for the female to pass through but too small for the male. This allows the female to enter the breeding compartment or flee from it. A hole about $\frac{3}{8}$ inch (1 cm.) in diameter is about right for a standard-sized female.

The two fish, when ready to mate, display and counter-display with a building of frenzy toward the mating embrace. With immature or inexperienced pairs, this may involve false tries. However, if both fish are in good condition and the

Illus. 36. This red male Betta is guarding his nest and watching for a suitable female.

Illus. 37. A female swims under the nest and begins her fin display and undulation in initial courting, even though she may not be fully ready to mate. The male makes a driving sideways display in a beginning effort to encircle the female and mate.

female is filled with eggs and large enough to accommodate the male, they will get together. The male will stay under the nest fairly near the surface and continue to display his breeding colors.

Illus. 38. The male Paradise Fish takes up a position just below the under surface of the nest, the female undulates and quivers at a point an inch or two below the nest and the male seeks to enwrap her with his body.

Illus. 39. The male draws his body into a tight loop around the female. As he tightens his grip he spins the female completely over until her vent is facing upward toward the nest, and his vent is in close proximity.

41

Illus. 40. As the two embracing fish fall slowly through the water, the eggs are released from the female vent and the sperm from the male vent. The eggs are fertilized immediately and, after a few seconds, begin to float upward in the water.

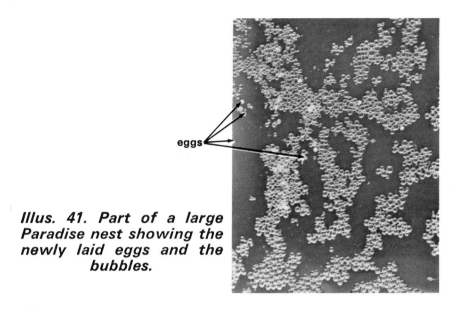

eggs

Illus. 41. Part of a large Paradise nest showing the newly laid eggs and the bubbles.

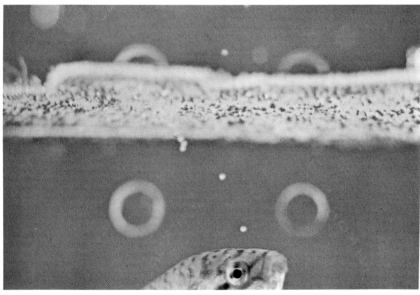

Illus. 42. A male Paradise Fish plucks and expels eggs from the nest. While most of the eggs will remain live and developing, infertile or imperfect ones will burst with this type of circulation, and from attacks by micro-organisms.

Illus. 43. A male Betta is caring for his very young fry. The arrow is pointing at a young hatchling about to be picked up by its father.

3. Breeding

Although the breeding activities of the Paradise and Betta are virtually identical, there are differences and it is necessary to look at both.

The eggs of the Betta are slightly heavier than water and sink slowly, to be caught by the male in his mouth, and gently blown into the nest along with a quantity of bubbles. After hatching, the young fishes dart about erratically to be caught and blown back into the nest by the male.

The Paradise eggs are lighter than water and rise slowly to the nest. With a fairly strong light at an oblique angle from the water surface, it is possible to see eggs in a tank in the bubble nest. Even though the eggs of the Paradise and some other Anabantoids float, the male fishes usually pluck them from the surface and circulate them in their mouths before expelling them back into the nest with more bubbles.

A microscopic examination will show that the water is full of tiny organisms which will approach the surface of the eggs and seek for some entrance through the outer membrane. Here and there, an infertile egg or one that has some imperfection will be attacked and devoured by these tiny invaders.

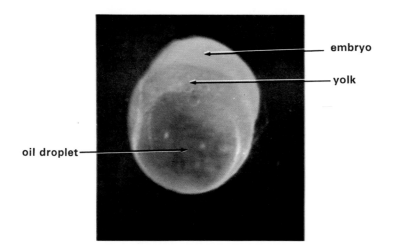

embryo

yolk

oil droplet

Illus. 44. This newly laid Paradise egg shows the two poles, the animal at the upper end, the vegetal, or yolk, at the lower end. The large sphere at the bottom is an oil droplet. This is the flotation mechanism of the developing embryo. The Betta egg has a greatly reduced oil droplet and tends to sink at all stages of development.

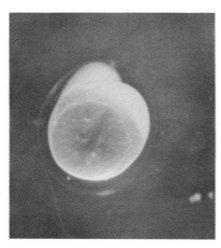

Illus. 45. In this first cleavage of a Paradise egg, note the shadow of the first cleavage furrow. $\frac{1}{2}$ hour.

These organisms break down or reduce the dead animal tissue of the eggs to simpler organic materials which support the life of many other microscopic plants and animals. Because of their role in the life of the aquatic system, they are called reducer-organisms. The constant circulation of water over the eggs washes off the reducers and also provides fresh oxygen to the eggs.

Anabantoids have elaborate parental habits that will naturally cull out those individuals which do not hatch or which hatch imperfectly. Out of the initial 100 to 600 eggs as few as 50 will develop under the parentage of a constantly supervising father fish. His handling and picking reduces the fry, so that only the fittest survive. If removed to an incubator or fry-tank without a father fish, as many as 90 per cent will hatch, but they will not be as large or strong as a natural population. Within a few days, the difference in the rate of growth will become evident, with some fishes progressing much more rapidly than others. In time this difference will result in the smaller fry being cannibalized.

Fertilization

Fertilization occurs almost instantaneously as the eggs are passed from the female vent and sprayed with sperm. For this reason, the early development proceeds at surprising speed. The first eggs laid and fertilized may appear 4 or 5 hours before the last eggs in the same spawning. This is one of the reasons it is hard to give precise dates and ages of hatchlings. Since the fry shown in the illustrations here were raised in a specially constructed incubator, fairly accurate times are given. All are dated from time of fertilization. Although there is an optimum temperature, there is really little varia-

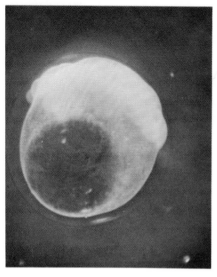

Illus. 46. In the early blastula of the Paradise, the cells are advancing over the surface and out along the edges of the yolk. 1¾ hours.

tion in the speed of development of eggs at one temperature and those at another.

The blastodisc is a flattened region at one end of the egg where the first cells will form. This shows the first sign of fertilization, and it takes place about 15 to 18 minutes after

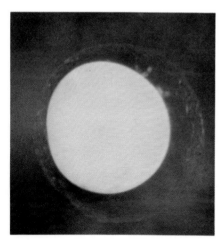

Illus. 47. Late blastula of a Betta egg. 4 hours.

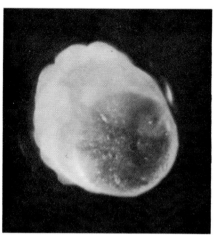

Illus. 48. The blastoderm, like a hollow cup, now covers a third of the yolk. The cellular mass is beginning to lengthen into one axis, and various furrows and ridges are beginning to appear in the surface of this Paradise embryo. 6 hours.

the egg is laid. In another 10 to 12 minutes, the first division or cleavage occurs.

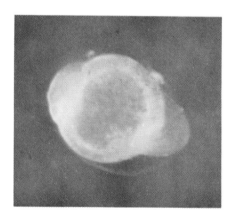

Illus. 49. Now a true fish embryo is distinguishable, with head and back-caudal areas differentiated. Three quarters of the yolk is surrounded by the developing embryo. The oil glob is greatly diminished, neural tissue is starting to become distinguished, and the heart and circulatory system are visible. 12 hours.

49

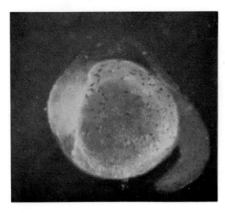

Illus. 50. The optic area is beginning to shade, and the caudal region is starting to form in the embryo. Also, the otolith is beginning to form. 20 hours.

egg membrane

eye buds

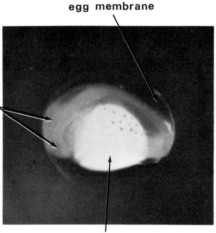

Illus. 51. This Betta embryo shows small oil droplets with fairly complete otic (ear) and optic (eye) systems. 24 hours.

yolk

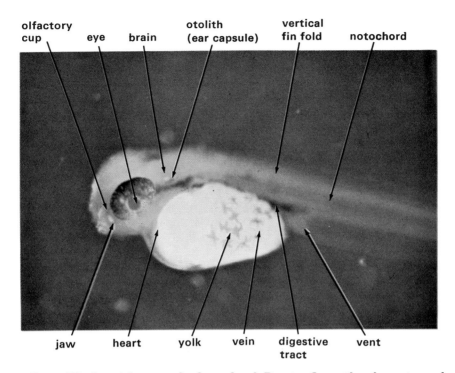

olfactory cup   eye   brain   otolith (ear capsule)   vertical fin fold   notochord

jaw   heart   yolk   vein   digestive tract   vent

Illus. 52. In this newly hatched Betta fry, the heart and circulation become apparent, but this fry is still borne by oil sacs. 32 hours.

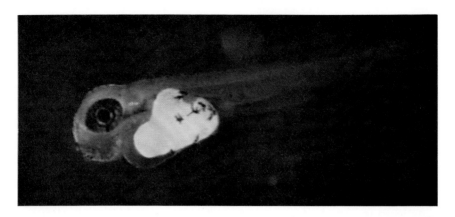

Illus. 53. The Betta fry is rapidly absorbing the yolk and becoming a self-feeder. Heart, eye movement and some simple swimming movements are advancing rapidly. The swim bladder has begun to form. 50 hours.

Early Growth

The development of the accessory breathing organ in the Anabantoids is nowhere near being fully understood. It appears as though in the Betta and the Paradise, the organ develops when the fry are 4 to 5 mm. in length. There is some evidence to support the contention that this is the first stage at which the fry can effectively break through the surface tension of the water. It is also a fact that not all adult fishes have the same accessory organ capacity, and no doubt there is even more variation between individuals in the fry.

Many young fish succumb during their first 21 to 30 days. There are two reasons for this: (1) The yolk supply is long gone and the fish starve in tanks without enough of the smaller copepods, the small shrimps and minute water

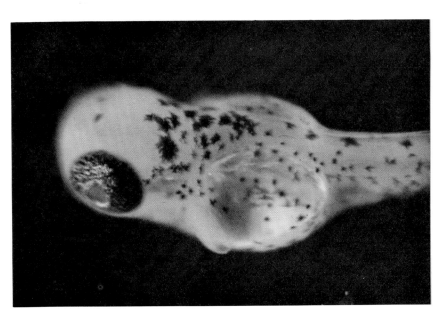

Illus. 54. Although this Paradise fry is fully formed and fully swimming its pectoral fin buds are just developing, and its gill slits are only starting to become functional. 60 hours.

crustaceans upon which the larvae feed in their natural habitat. At this stage, the young fish are too large to eat microbes or one-celled fare and must eat the slightly larger shelled and arthropod water organisms. (2) It is at this time that the accessory breathing organ is being formed. If the temperature of the water and the moisture-laden air above are not both fairly warm and fairly even, the fry cannot survive. This calls for a relatively low water level and the tight-fitting glass cover.

The Betta and Paradise fry are very small and delicate and are a real challenge to the aquarist to keep alive. Many have found that a small bit of hard-boiled egg yolk squeezed into the water through clean white gauze will give sufficient food for the tiny fishes.

As a rule, a bare-slate-bottom tank with very old water and subdued sunlight is best. The addition of a fair layering of floating plants aids both mature fishes and fry.

Both the Paradise and the Betta are fascinating to observe in the tank, and a challenge to keep, breed, and raise properly. Their interesting habits and adaptations are well worth the effort.

Illus. 55. The eyes of the Paradise fry now focus and it pursues and devours infusorians in the water. The fry is developed enough to seek shelter and stay in corners and other recesses of the aquarium. 80 hours.

Illus. 56. The Betta fry at one week old spend most of their daylight hours pursuing microscopic food.

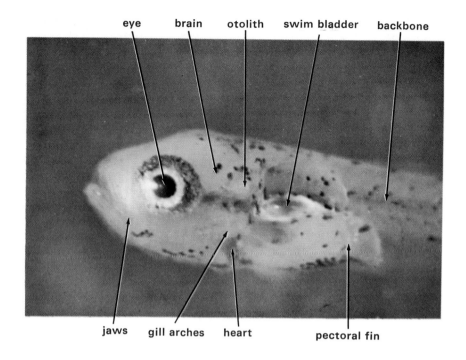

eye   brain   otolith   swim bladder   backbone

jaws   gill arches   heart   pectoral fin

Illus. 57. The Betta at 14 days shows the developing organs of the head and the breathing organs.

Illus. 58. At 14 days, the Betta's accessory breathing organ is developing, and the fish will surface, but not make air exchange at the surface. It is 3.5 mm. long.

Illus. 59. The Betta fry begins to show adult form and pigmentation at 21 days.

*Illus. 60. A weed-choked tropical water hole, the usual
habitat of the Betta and Paradise Fishes.*

4. Ecology

The breathing apparatus of the Anabantoids fits them for
life in shallow water with poor oxygen content. Reports
from Southeast Asia confirm this characteristic of their
habitat. Their slow movements and strong pectoral fins
suggest a slow-moving or still-water environment. Both of
these suppositions are correct. In their native state, these
fishes live in small weed-choked drainage ditches in and
around rice patties and similar environments of standing

water. Not only are they fitted by form to their environment, but also in function. In some ways their behavior is even more complex than their anatomy.

The building of nests and the defending of territories is usually found in fishes with limited environments, where not all males can reproduce the species and competition for mates and mating areas has been the outcome. What better and more complete competition than a battle to the death or ouster of immature or weaker males? In the same fashion, eggs and fry raised in oxygen-depleted water must have some support to keep them as close to the surface of the water as possible. The bubble nest anchored with floating plants answers the need perfectly.

Many other subtle aspects of the Betta's life history and behavior are not so well known or are imperfectly understood. The more observers, however, the more questions will be answered. From many points of view then, these small fishes are a remarkable part of the wonders of creation.

Index